AF588180

Mindful Breathing

Mindful Breathing

Find more calm and greater joy in every day

SARAH RUDELL BEACH

CICO BOOKS

This edition published in 2026 by CICO Books
an imprint of Ryland Peters & Small Ltd
20–21 Jockey's Fields
London WC1R 4BW
www.rylandpeters.com
Email: euregulations@rylandpeters.com

First published in 2020 as *And Breathe...*
Text adapted from *Mindful Moments for Busy Moms*, published in 2018

10 9 8 7 6 5 4 3 2 1

A CIP record for this book is available from the British Library.
US Library of Congress CIP data has been applied for.

ISBN: 978-1-80065-647-5

Printed in China

Editor: Dawn Bates
Designer: Eliana Holder
Illustrator: Clare Nicholas

Commissioning editor: Kristine Pidkameny
Art director: Sally Powell
Head of production: Patricia Harrington
Publishing manager: Penny Craig
Publisher: Cindy Richards

The authorised representative in the EEA is
Authorised Rep Compliance Ltd.,
Ground Floor. 71 Lower Baggot Street,
Dublin, D01 P593, Ireland
www.arccompliance.com

FOR *Abby*
AND *Liam*

I LOVE YOU TO THE MOON AND BACK. AND I LOVE BEING YOUR MOM.

contents

INTRODUCTION

Sometimes we just need to stop, take a moment, *and breathe*... When we're mindful of our breathing, with a full inhale and a full exhale, we activate the body's relaxation response, which has a calming effect. In this collection of mindfulness practices, meditations, and mantras, you will learn many ways to be mindful and achieve greater calm, balance, and joy in your life. So what is mindfulness?

Mindfulness is purposeful awareness of the present moment, which allows us to accept what is happening right now. We are aware of our thoughts and feelings, and we are able to pause and respond skillfully to challenges, instead of reacting based on unconscious habits. Mindfulness brings us into the now—allowing us to see the goodness (or okayness) in the most ordinary of experiences. It helps us regulate our emotional responses and soothe our nervous systems. It allows us to find peace and stability, so we can experience nourishing self-care. Mindfulness helps us keep our cool and stops us from losing our ... *ahem, stuff* every day.

PURPOSEFUL AWARENESS OF THE MOMENT

Sometimes we're paying attention, but not on purpose. It's the honk of another car, or a child yelling for attention the tenth time that day, that jolts us out of our distraction.

Mindfulness is paying attention on *purpose*. It is an intentional awareness of the sensations, thoughts, feelings, and experiences of the present moment.

We spend a lot of our time thinking about the past or planning for the future. When we are mindful, we are paying attention to our present moment experience. For example, if you barely get a response when you hand your boss a 30-page report you've been working hard on or if you serve dinner and your child immediately responds with, "But I hate chicken," you would pay attention to your body's response—your racing pulse, your clenched jaw, the anger rising in your chest. You wouldn't stop all those responses, you would simply become *aware* of them. But instead of letting that anger lead to a long-winded speech about your continuous acts of sacrifice for your work or family, or a build-up of resentment, mindfulness would help you …

ACCEPT WHAT IS HAPPENING WITH CURIOSITY AND WITHOUT JUDGMENT

You would allow the present moment to be what it is … because it's already here and happening. You wouldn't have to *like* it. Instead, you'd accept it without judgment, and get curious: I wonder if my boss has a lot on her plate at the moment? Why is my child getting upset? Did something happen today? Why am I getting upset? Did something happen today?

When I first started practicing mindfulness, I thought not judging things meant I had to *like* everything in every moment and think that everything that happened was amazing and wonderful, but mindfulness is about being with the entire range of our human experience, whether it is pleasant or unpleasant. So once you've noticed what's happening, gotten curious about it, and accepted it without judgment, you would …

KNOW WHAT YOU ARE THINKING AND FEELING

You would recognize the feelings of anger, resentment, and righteous indignation. You wouldn't fight these thoughts and feelings, you'd just observe them, watching them increase in intensity and then, most likely, subside. Then you would …

PAUSE AND RESPOND SKILLFULLY

You would pause and breathe and instead of falling into your default mode (an epic sermon about your mama-martyrdom or a negative train of thought where you're *so* getting a new job), you would lovingly remind your child of the last time she ate this meal and how much she enjoyed it or wish your boss a good evening and say, "Let me know your thoughts on that report when you get a moment." It's not a huge victory, but responding in this way feels amazing. And, really, it is kind of a huge deal, because what often drains us are the daily small battles, frustrations, and indignities.

SO HOW CAN YOU LEARN TO DO THIS?

One of the most important things about mindfulness is that it is a *practice*. It's something we must cultivate—we can't just read a book, decide to appreciate mindfulness and peacefulness and attentiveness from now on, and expect things to change, any more than we can read a book about exercise, decide to appreciate sweat and movement, and then expect to be fitter.

We have to practice. Mindfulness is like a muscle, something that will grow stronger the more we use it. The more we practice pausing, the better we will get at it. The more we practice being fully present with our breath, the better we will become at being fully present with our loved ones. The more aware we become of our thought patterns, the less we'll be driven by them, and we'll be able to change those reactive habits that aren't serving us well. And, according to the research, we'll experience less stress and greater joy.

AND HOW DO YOU FIND THE TIME?

When you're really busy, you might think taking 5 minutes to meditate just isn't worth it, because then you'll be even more behind schedule. But we often "earn back" the time we spend in mindfulness practice. Spending a few minutes in quiet stillness creates a calm and focus that will help you be more productive and efficient throughout your day.

A famous Zen saying tells us that if we don't have 1 hour for meditation in our day, then we need at least 2 hours. I don't know many people who have 2 hours for daily meditation, but I'm pretty sure you have 5 minutes! (And if you don't have 5, you probably need 10.) With mindfulness, consistency of practice is far more important than the duration of your practice. Even 5 minutes a day of breathing in attentive silence will help you cultivate greater calm, focus, and patience.

Although it's important to create time for mindfulness practice in your day, it's also important not to make mindfulness just another item on your to-do list, a chore that must be completed. Mindfulness should be a "get to," not a "have to." Think of ways that you can ritualize your practice—maybe lighting a candle or listening to soothing music—so that your time feels special and set apart from the rest of your day. Allow your time for mindfulness to be a gift you give yourself. You are fully *on* for most of your day—taking in information, responding to the world, moving through space, navigating your surroundings—and all that time being *on* takes its toll on your energy, clarity, and presence. Think of meditation as your time *not* to be on—not to have to respond, engage, or move. To simply *be*.

HOW TO USE THIS BOOK

This book is intended to provide both guidance and inspiration for your mindfulness practice. You'll discover lots of different ways to bring mindfulness into your busy days. Think of this book as a menu, not an all-you-can-eat buffet. Sample the exercises that appeal to you, experiment with them in the laboratory of your own life, and see what works for you. If a particular practice brings you some ease and comfort, you can come back for seconds. Honor your feelings and intuition—if a mantra or meditation practice doesn't feel right to you, modify it or don't do it at all. You can't do all of them every day, nor should you even try!

If you're new to mindfulness, I recommend you start with Chapter 1, as it contains many introductory practices and meditations to get you started on the basics. You could try a different meditation or mantra each day or read the whole book straight through and compile your own mindfulness menu. It's entirely up to you.

See if you can approach mindfulness with an attitude of playfulness—play with these practices, see what resonates with you, and consider how you can integrate mindfulness into your life as an important component of your self-care.

A FEW HELPFUL NOTES

1. I am often asked how we should breathe in meditation. Open mouth or closed mouth? In through the nose or out through the nose? The simple answer is just to let your breath be natural. You don't need to try to breathe in any particular way—in fact, trying to force the breath to be a certain way can create more stress and agitation! Simply focus on what your breath is like, in your body, right now. Breathe in the way that is most comfortable for you.

2. Some meditations begin with an instruction to "Close your eyes ..." Read the meditation a few times, and then close your eyes and practice. You could also have someone read them to you, or you could dictate them into your phone and use the recording to practice.

3. This is a book about mindfulness and meditation. What's the difference? Mindfulness is a broad term, referring to our ability to attend to the present moment no matter what we are doing. It is something we can cultivate throughout our day, even as we engage in other activities. When I use the word "meditation," I am referring to the formal practice in which we sit (or lie) down, close our eyes, and deliberately bring our attention to a particular aspect of our experience (the breath, for example). Think of meditation sessions as the formal training you do for a few minutes every day to strengthen your mindfulness muscles. The more you practice meditation, the more you will notice an improvement in your ability to be mindful throughout your day.

4. If you fall asleep during your meditation time, that's okay. It's just a nap. If you fell asleep quickly, you probably needed a nap far more than you needed meditation. You can adjust your posture and choose a time of day to practice when you'll be most alert, but it's also totally fine to be so present with your sleepiness that you fall asleep.

5. You may think you are "bad" at mindfulness and meditation because your mind wanders away from the present moment. But when you notice it happening, that's great news! It means you are becoming more aware of the activity of your mind, so you are absolutely doing it right.

6. The mantras can be used in a variety of ways. You can silently repeat them in your head during formal practice, or whenever you need them throughout the day, or say them out loud if you find it helpful. Once you discover the mantras that most resonate with you, perhaps write them down on a post-it, or on your favorite stationery, and fix them where you will see them regularly (on a mirror, refrigerator, etc.).

CHAPTER 1

Begin

MINDFULNESS PRACTICES

The meditations and mantras in this chapter will help you to ease into a mindfulness practice. You can use these exercises "on the go" as you need them, or you can make them part of a formal mindfulness time each day. By taking small steps, you will gradually cultivate greater awareness, presence, and calm. Try to spend 5–10 minutes every day experimenting with different exercises. You'll soon discover the ones that work most effectively for you.

A *Short* AND *Sweet*

SIMPLE MEDITATION

Meditation does not need to be mysterious, complicated, or time-consuming. Set a timer for 5 minutes, and allow your eyes to close. Now count your breaths—begin counting "1" on the inhale, then "2" on the exhale, and so on, until you reach 10, and then start over again at 1. If your mind wanders away from counting your breath (which it will most likely do), just start over again at 1. You may start over 73 times in 5 minutes, and that's okay. Just continue focusing on your breath until the timer goes off, and then see how you feel when you're done!

MANTRA

WITH EACH BREATH

I RELEASE TENSION.

BE IN *This Moment*

It's so easy for our thoughts to get pulled into the future or stuck in the past. When you notice your thoughts racing forward to the next moment, or dwelling on some previous moment, see if you can bring yourself to *this* moment. Right here, right now. What is happening now? What is needed of you *now*?

KEEP AN *Open Mind*

Try to approach your practice without any preconceived ideas of how it's supposed to look or feel or be. You may find that your practice is relaxing, but that isn't the "goal." One day it might be relaxing. The next day it might be boring. And then the next day you just feel hungry and your back hurts. And then the day after that, you love it. Just notice whatever is happening when you practice— if you hate it, notice that you're hating it. If you are tense and irritated, notice that you are tense and irritated. If you think you are really bad at mindfulness, notice that you are thinking you are bad at mindfulness!

Scan YOUR BODY

Close your eyes, and as you breathe, gently scan your body. See if you can identify somewhere in your body that feels pleasant, perhaps a sense of relaxation in the face, or warmth in the hands. Spend some time with this sensation. How do you know it is pleasant? What is pleasant about it? How does it feel to spend time focusing on a part of the body that feels good?

Then do the same thing with an unpleasant sensation: what is it, how do you know it's unpleasant, and what happens when you bring awareness to it? There's no "right" or "wrong" way to do this meditation, but you might notice that 1) you have some choice in where you place your attention, and 2) what you pay attention to can impact your present moment experience.

FIVE SENSES *Meditation*

Close your eyes, and identify one thing you can notice, right at this moment, with each of your five senses. What do you smell? What sounds do you hear? Where is your body making contact with the world? What do you visualize? Can you taste anything? Your awareness of your sensory experiences brings you directly into the present moment.

Tune in TO YOUR BREATH

All day long, your body performs the miraculous task of keeping you alive, with no real involvement on your part. Your lungs breathe, your stomach digests, your heart beats, and your neurons fire. So when you practice mindfulness, you don't need to bring a lot of extra effort to it. You don't have to force the breath—just let the body breathe, and pay attention.

Ask, "WHAT IS THIS?"

You can ask this question at any moment of your day. What is this? "Ah, this is anger ..." "Ah, this is an overworked partner." "Ah, this is resentment." Mindfulness is simply about clearly knowing what *this* is.

FIND YOUR *Anchor*

A helpful way to begin mindfulness meditation is to identify an anchor that you can bring your attention to. This can be your breath, the sensations in your body, or the sounds in your environment. It doesn't really matter which anchor you choose—it's simply there to provide your busy mind with a place to return to when it wanders. Just like a boat might drift away a bit before being gently tugged back into place, your mind will float along on a thought until your anchor brings you back to the present moment. For the next few moments, choose an anchor for your attention, such as your breath, a part of your body, or a sound, and close your eyes. When your mind wanders, keep coming back to your anchor. Again and again.

BE *Effortless*

Simply sit in meditation and let your bones and gravity do most of the work of holding you in place. Allow your upper body to be upright, with your head resting gently on the spine. Roll your shoulders up and back to open up your chest, and release the tension in as many muscles as you can. The work your body does to hold you in various postures throughout the day doesn't account for a huge caloric burn, but it still takes energy. The gentle posture of meditation is soothing because it reduces the effort of your body.

MANTRA

I CAN BE HERE NOW.

Relax YOUR FACE

This simple exercise will help you to become mindful of any tension you hold in your face and help you relax. Take a deep breath, and bring your awareness to your face. Unclench your teeth, and allow your jaw to relax or even drop open. Soften the muscles around your mouth. Release any holding in your cheeks. Soften your eyes; unfurrow your brow. Feel your breath gently entering your nose, and then gliding over your lips as you exhale. Allow your entire face to be soft and at rest.

TAKE *Three Breaths*

No matter how busy your day is, you have time to pause for three deep breaths. You don't even need to close your eyes. Wherever you are, you can stop for a moment and bring your attention to your breath. On the first breath, focus on what it feels like as you inhale, as you bring nourishing oxygen to your body. On the second breath, focus on the exhale, and enjoy the soothing effects of the out-breath. On the third breath, breathe in what you need—perhaps love, energy, and wisdom—and release any feelings you don't need—perhaps resentment, worry, and anger.

Notice JUDGMENTS

The primary task of your brain is to keep you alive, so it spends much of its time judging things: "Is this okay? Am I safe? Should I approach or avoid?" Most of the time, you don't even know this is happening … and this is where you can get into trouble. Your mind starts judging a situation, and before you even realize what's happened, you've jumped to all sorts of (likely inaccurate) conclusions about it. For today, see if you can notice all the times you are judging things ("I like this, I don't like that"), and see what impact those judgments have on your experience.

PRACTICE WHEN IT IS *Easy*

Some days, spending 10 minutes (or even 5 minutes!) just breathing might seem like a complete waste of time. You can probably think of about 18 other things you could be doing during those 10 minutes. But that time of breathing … resting … stopping … settling … calming … is actually time incredibly well spent. If you practice mindfulness when it's easy, you'll be able to do it when it's hard. When you hit a tough moment in your day, you'll know how to pause and calm yourself down. When it gets hard, you'll know what to do.

FIND THE *Roots* OF THE *Tree*

We often refer to our minds as "monkey minds," because they jump from thought to thought as often as monkeys leap from branch to branch. As you practice mindfulness, you'll start to get familiar with the branches your monkey mind likes to swing around on. You might notice the same thought patterns and worries appear again and again in meditation. I like to think of this as finally starting to see the *roots* of the tree your monkey mind keeps circling. And once you've identified those roots, you've discovered some helpful information! Perhaps a thought keeps popping up because there's something you need to resolve. Noticing these repetitive thought patterns is not a problem in meditation—it's the beginning of insight.

MANTRA

I WILL FOCUS ON WHAT I CAN CONTROL.

KNOW THAT IT IS JUST *This*

Whatever you're doing, just do it, and know that you are doing it. Mindfulness is knowing you're ...

Just cleaning
Just driving
Just eating
Just singing
Just cooking
Just walking
Just talking
Just sitting
Just reading
Just being

Check YOUR REACTIONS

Every feeling you have fundamentally boils down to the question of whether you are drawn to approach or avoid something. Today, set an intention to notice your immediate reactions to the events of your day. Notice if there is a visceral sense of pleasantness or unpleasantness, and if this instant assessment begins to impact the thoughts you are having about what's happening. You don't need to get upset with yourself for reacting to things so quickly—it's what your body was designed to do. But see if you can notice how these immediate feelings of attraction or revulsion impact your mood, and your behavior.

MANTRA

PEACE IS AVAILABLE TO ME IN EVERY MOMENT OF THE DAY.

See the World AS A CHILD SEES THE WORLD

Children approach the world with a true beginner's mind—everything is new to them! They are fascinated by things such as onions, insects, leaves, belly buttons, water bottles, and faces. They truly see what they are looking at, with curiosity and delight. What would it be like if you looked at the world this way today?

Listen MINDFULLY

Close your eyes, and just listen. You don't have to "work hard" at hearing—just allow the sounds in your environment to come to you. Can you hear any sounds from within your body? Do you hear your breath? What can you hear in this room? Outside this room? If you don't really notice any sounds, just note that. Any time we bring our attention to the present moment, we cultivate focus and stillness. And sometimes, silence.

Feel THE GRAVITATIONAL PULL

Wherever you are right now, take a deep breath and feel the gentle pull of gravity, keeping you grounded and stable. Feel your body sinking into the chair or couch or bed, or feel your feet firmly on the earth. Notice the position of your body in relationship to the space around you. At any moment of the day, you can find stability by becoming aware of gravity.

"Soften"

I think this is sometimes the only mantra we need. *Soften.* Release the tension in your neck, shoulders, jaw, forehead, hands, eyes, legs, chest, torso, your entire body. Release your resistance. Soften your heart, allowing it to feel expansive and open. Meet this moment with softness and ease, meet your loved ones with softness and ease, meet your thoughts with softness and ease. Take a deep breath, and soften. Repeat the mantra "Soften."

Check It Out

This is a helpful mantra to remind yourself to check in with yourself throughout your day. Just tell yourself to "check it out": where are you, what are you doing, what are you thinking, how are you feeling? Just be present for a moment, and check it out.

Learn TO SINGLE-TASK

Everyone seems to pride themselves these days on multitasking, but the fact is, no one is actually good at it. The word "multitask" is a computer word, because computers can do all sorts of things, such as crunching numbers and sending emails and surfing the Internet, all at the same time. Humans cannot. So go easy on yourself. Do one thing at a time today. Send that email, *then* work out your grocery list, *then* make that call, *then* sit down and have a coffee, mindfully. You'll get a lot more done, and feel a lot better, when you allow yourself to single-task.

Tune In To Your Thoughts

(BUT DO NOT ALWAYS BELIEVE THEM)

Thoughts can be intense and persuasive, but most of the time, they're not true—they're just stories and interpretations and misinterpretations. Our thoughts are with us constantly throughout the day, and often we're completely unaware of them and how much they influence our mood and behavior. Today, see if you can bring your awareness to your thoughts, just knowing *what* you are thinking *when* you are thinking it. And remember that you don't have to believe everything you think! You may notice that sometimes you have a thought such as "I'm not good at my job." With mindfulness, you can remind yourself that it's just a thought. You can say, "Right now, I'm just thinking I'm not good at my job." This subtle shift in how you approach your thoughts can make a dramatic change in your day.

"I AM *Aware* AND IN THE *Moment*"

Awareness, as hard as it can be to cultivate sometimes, is actually your natural state. With mindfulness, you're not trying to manufacture some extra-ordinary blissful experience; you're simply resting in the awareness that is always available to you, in any moment. You can be aware of the heat of the sun on your face. You can be aware of a voice, the story someone's telling you, and the expressions on that person's face. This, too, is mindfulness. Repeat the mantra "I Am Aware and In the Moment."

KNOW YOUR *Default Setting*

We all have a set of default thoughts and behaviors that we tend to enact when we get frustrated or overwhelmed or angry—heavy sighing, loud yelling, quiet crying, self-critical thinking ... With mindfulness, you can become more aware of these unthinking, knee-jerk reactions, and you can start to interrupt them with a moment of presence. Then you can respond with a wise choice, based on what's actually happening, instead of relying on ingrained habits that don't always serve you. Throughout your day, notice your default settings and reactions, and see if you can make these unconscious behaviors conscious.

"I Am Perfect AS I Am"

Mindfulness is not about self-improvement. In fact, the fundamental insight of mindfulness is that you already have everything you need, right now in this moment. Right now you can breathe, you can find the clarity to see things as they are, and you can cultivate the wisdom to respond skillfully to what is in front of you. Mindfulness practice is not about changing who you are or trying to be "better"; it's about learning to trust yourself as you find new ways to meet the challenges that arise each day. Repeat the mantra "I Am Perfect as I Am."

FIND THE MOST Important THING

Perhaps one of the most enduring questions of the human experience is, "What is the most important thing I must do?" Russian novelist Leo Tolstoy had a great answer to that question over a century ago in his story "The Three Questions." When a king asked a wise man, "What is the most important thing I must do?", the wise man told him, "The thing you're doing *now*." Whatever you are doing right now, *that* is the most important thing. What would your days, and your life, be like if you did *every* thing as if it were the only, and the most important, thing to do?

BE *Openly* AWARE

In many mindfulness exercises, we deliberately place our focus on a particular anchor, such as the breath (see, for example, page 19). However, with open awareness, we allow our attention to rest on whatever happens to be present. In this practice, you can close your eyes, begin breathing, and *just* notice—a thought, a cough, a twitch in your hand, a phone ringing, a memory, a softening in the jaw, the sound of a clock. It's not necessarily letting your mind wander, because you are paying attention, but you're also not constantly bringing your awareness back to your breath. Your only intention here is to be present to whatever arises. See if you can try this practice today, simply allowing your mind to rest on whatever captures your attention.

MANTRA

I CAN CALM MYSELF WITH A DEEP BREATH.

Breathe Out

When you breathe in, you activate the body's sympathetic nervous system (the "activating" and energizing part of the nervous system), and when you breathe out, you activate the parasympathetic nervous system, the so-called "relaxation response" of the body. One way to take advantage of the soothing effects of the out-breath is to lengthen your exhale deliberately; for example, you can breathe in for four counts, and then breathe out for six counts. When you need a moment of soothing today, take a deep breath in and really linger on the exhale.

BE OUT OF CONTROL

Life is much less stressful when we can make peace with things that are outside of our control, such as that traffic jam, a loved one's bad mood, the weather. For this meditation, close your eyes and practice not controlling any part of your experience. Just allow your breath to be natural, without trying to breathe in any particular way. If thoughts arise, just let them be there, without stopping or engaging them. If you notice sensations in your body, see if you can allow them to be there, without scratching an itch or adjusting your posture or anything else you might be tempted to do to exert your will on your experience. Just practice being out of control.

Know YOUR WHY

Why do you want to bring mindfulness and meditation into your life? There are lots of reasons to do it, but the most important one is YOURS. Why are you here, right now, reading these words? What do you need in your life? Peace, presence, comfort, connection, serenity, compassion, or all of the above? It can be hard to make changes to your habitual ways of acting, and it's even harder if you don't have a clear sense of purpose. Spend some time today reflecting on your why: *why do you want to practice mindfulness?* On the days when it's hard to find the time or energy to practice, your why will bring you back.

CREATE *Spaciousness*

Feeling *spacious* is the opposite of feeling tense, closed-off, and contracted. Take a few deep breaths and see if you can bring some spaciousness and expansion to your body—open up your chest, spread out your fingers and toes, stretch your arms above your head, and open your jaw. Take a few deep breaths and imagine each breath is an invitation to greater openness, relaxation, acceptance, and tranquility.

Notice YOUR RACE CAR MIND

It's totally okay when you notice you have not just a *racing* mind, but a *race car mind*: a mind that whips around the track at ridiculous speeds, and never seems to need refueling. Like that race car, your mind gets stuck on a track, revisiting the same terrain over and over again, instead of venturing somewhere new. When you notice your *race car mind*, see if you can get out of the driver's seat (because this vehicle will go on without you), and simply stand in the grass in the middle of the track. See if you can just watch the speeding car without being thrown about on hairpin turns, without your heart racing as fast as those wheels spin. See if you can be the observer of your thoughts, and not the driver.

TAKE A *Pause*

We often bring our attention to the breath in mindfulness because it is always with us, and directing our attention to the bodily experience of breathing gets us out of our heads and creates some distance from our thoughts. One way to practice mindful breathing is with an ever-so-slight pause between the in-breath and the out-breath, and between the out-breath and the in-breath. Notice the sensations of this liminal moment. Practice attending to the distinct sensations of the in-breath compared to those of the out-breath. Can you experience breathing in and breathing out as two separate events?

MANTRA

I CAN NOTICE WHAT IS HAPPENING RIGHT NOW.

LABEL YOUR *Thoughts*

Noting is a powerful mindfulness practice for working with thoughts. When you notice a thought arise, either during your formal practice or as you're going about your day, see if you can acknowledge the thought with a simple label, such as "worrying," "judging," "remembering," or "planning." Don't worry about getting the label right—just "thinking" will do, too. In this way, you can notice the thought without getting entirely wrapped up in its contents. You can notice if the thought is loud or soft, pleasant or unpleasant, or short-lived or persistent. For today, practice labeling your thoughts, and then see what happens to them when you step back and don't get entangled in them.

ASK *"How do I know?"*

A helpful practice for cultivating a deeper awareness of your emotions is to ask yourself, "How do I know I am angry?" (or whatever you happen to be feeling.) Maybe you know you're angry because your jaw is clenched, or because the space between your eyes is pulsing, or because you have a strong desire to throw something. Whatever it is, ask yourself, "How do I know this is my experience?" This isn't about getting a "right" answer; it's simply a way to cultivate greater understanding.

Don't Wait FOR THE WORLD TO GET QUIET AROUND YOU

I once taught mindfulness to elementary students in a very noisy and chaotic after-school program. Sometimes the kids would get frustrated when we were trying to practice our mindfulness and everyone else was being loud and distracting. I told them, "If we wait for the world to get quiet around us, we're going to be waiting for a very long time." Mindfulness isn't something we practice only when the conditions are perfect—it's something that helps us create peace and quiet in ourselves as we move through a noisy and chaotic world.

HANDLE YOUR *Feelings*

As if emotions weren't complicated enough, we also have feelings about our feelings! We tell ourselves that we "shouldn't" be resentful of our partner or frustrated with a co-worker, or that certain emotions, such as anger or frustration, are not acceptable. When you notice this happening, remind yourself that all emotional experiences are simply a part of the human condition, and that whatever you are feeling is okay. Anything that can be experienced can also be worked with, so take a deep breath and investigate your emotions, your needs, and what you could do to take care of yourself.

Note HOW YOU PAY ATTENTION

One of my absolute favorite quotes about mindfulness comes from neuroscientist Sam Harris in his book *Waking Up*. He writes, "How we pay attention to the present moment largely determines the character of our experience and, therefore, the quality of our lives." Your day—and your life—is made up of an infinite number of present moments. How will you meet them? Notice the quality of the attention you bring to your present moments: Are you focused? Curious? Engaged? Impatient? How does the way you pay attention to those moments change your experience? How does the way you pay attention to your loved ones change your interactions with them?

Telescope YOUR ATTENTION

Sometimes we must attend to one small part of our experience (such as reading a book or playing a game), and other times we need to zoom out and take in a great deal of information at once (when we're driving, for example). You can play with this telescoping of attention in your mindfulness practice. First, bring your attention to your breath and your body, and stay with that for a few minutes. Then see if you can expand your attention to your surroundings, noticing the air, sounds, and smells around you. Finally, try to expand your attention even further, extending out of the room and into the outside world, noticing any sounds or sense impressions, or simply imagine your awareness is expanding outward and upward toward the sky. Then you can play with bringing your attention back to the room, and finally to your breath.

Practice COHERENT BREATHING

Some amazing scientists studied the "most relaxing" rate of breathing, and discovered that it's about five or six breaths per minute (compared to the average adult breathing rate of 12–15 breaths per minute). To practice coherent breathing, you can use a timer, or you can simply count in your head as you breathe in and out. To breathe six times per minute, count to five on the inhale, using all 5 seconds for your breath. It's important to make the in-breath last for the full 5 seconds, as opposed to taking a quick breath in and holding it. Then count to five on the exhale, slowly releasing the breath. Try it for 2 minutes and see how it feels. Do you feel more relaxed?

MANTRA

I AM FOCUSED ON THIS TASK.

I CAN DO JUST THIS.

JUST *Note* GONE

Mindfulness teacher Shinzen Young describes a slightly more advanced mindfulness practice he calls "just note gone." It's an "advanced" practice because it's somewhat easy to notice what is here, and present, but much more difficult to notice what is NOT here. We often don't recognize when the headache goes away, or when the thought ends. For today, practice noting "gone." If you were aware of something, and then you eventually realize it's not there anymore, "just note gone." Don't worry about getting it at the instant it disappears; just acknowledge that what was once present has now shifted.

Listen TO YOUR BODY

Your emotions are almost always physical before they are conscious—there's a pit in your stomach, a trembling in your hands, or a new tension in your jaw that alerts you that something important is happening. Today, practice being aware of your body and the signals it sends. See if you can identify the unique markers of different emotions in your system, such as when you feel sad, angry, jealous, or happy. Cultivating this deep attunement with your body and its messages is a core component of emotional awareness.

Enjoy A MENTAL MASSAGE

Close your eyes, take a few deep breaths, and roll your shoulders back. Keeping your posture upright, allow yourself to release any tension in your neck and back. As you continue to focus on your breath, imagine someone gently placing her hands on the top of your head (you could even place your own hands there if you'd like). Imagine the feeling of warmth and soft pressure on your skull, and then pretend that her hands move to stroke your hair soothingly. Envision them lightly massaging your neck and shoulders, moving to exactly where you need relaxation. It might even help to think of a time you've had a pleasant massage or back rub, and remember the soothing sensations. Take a deep breath and savor this feeling of being nurtured and cared for.

Note AVOIDANCE

It's natural for our mindfulness practice to ebb and flow, to have times when we're committed to our daily meditation habit, and times when we just can't find our way to it. But if you notice a pattern of avoiding your mindfulness or meditation time, do some gentle inquiry to figure out why. Dodging your practice can be the focus of your practice! What stories are you telling yourself about why you're not making time for mindfulness? Are difficult thoughts or emotions arising when you meditate? Bring some curiosity and compassion to your avoidance, remind yourself why you started this practice in the first place, and see if you can identify what's standing in your way.

Check YOUR POSTURE

There is an amazing relationship between how we hold our body, and how we feel. If we stand upright, with our shoulders back and our feet grounded on the earth, we feel confident and powerful. Try experimenting right now with standing up tall and proud, and notice how that feels. Then allow yourself to slouch, let your head droop forward, and draw your feet together as your body folds in on itself. Do you notice a difference? For today, practice checking in with your posture. Are you in a position that conveys alertness and confidence? Can you make subtle shifts in your body and see how that feels?

MINDFUL MOMENT *Meditation*

Breathe in and notice any tension in the body.
Breathe out and release the tension.
Breathe in and notice if judgments or thoughts are present.
Breathe out and remember that thoughts are just thoughts.
Breathe in and notice any emotions that are present.
Breathe out and know that this emotion is not you.
Breathe in and smile.
Breathe out and relax.

Try NOT TO *Follow* THE THOUGHT

It's easy when a thought comes up in meditation to think, "This is really important—I need to address this thought before it goes away." Thoughts are seductive, and are great at convincing us that we must act upon them immediately. See if you can resist the temptation to interrupt your practice to chase a thought, jot down more to-dos, or solve a problem. Trust that the stillness and receptivity you cultivate in your mindfulness practice will allow a deeper knowing to emerge once you allow all the surface chatter in your mind to settle. Stay with your practice.

MANTRA

I AM NOT MY THOUGHTS.

CHAPTER 2

Starting the Day

MORNING PRACTICES

Mornings offer a bewildering array of experiences. One morning you may be able to linger in the sweetness and stillness of the first few moments of a day when the world has not yet demanded much of you. And then on other days the morning may be a chaotic blur—perhaps you didn't have a good night's sleep or you were woken early, or maybe your morning routine didn't run smoothly.

Mornings can be a great time to practice mindfulness, however, because no matter what the day has in store for you, you can begin with a few moments of mindful reflection that prepare you to meet the new day with intention and presence.

THE *First Moment* OF YOUR DAY

If you can, don't rush yourself out of bed in the morning. Feel the movement of your body, and consider your intention for the day (see page 50). If you have a few more seconds, take a deep breath in, welcoming the strength and energy you will need for your day, and then breathe out while you imagine releasing worries and tension and anything else you don't need today.

EMBODIED *Presence*

As you wake in the morning, can you become aware of the process of shifting from sleep to wakefulness? When you rouse from sleep, there is a brief experience of spaciousness, as consciousness is still a bit fuzzy in the movement from your dream state to awakening. Can you feel yourself "move back in" to your body? Can you sense this re-embodying that happens each morning? Set an intention today to be mindful of your body, bringing careful attention to movements and sensations as you move through your day. See if you can live fully in your body today.

Early Morning MEDITATION

If you can, wake up 10 minutes earlier than normal (or more if you'd like). Sit upright on a cushion or your couch or your bed, and set a timer for 10 minutes. Close your eyes and bring your attention to your breath. If you live with other people, notice what it feels like to be awake when everyone else is sleeping. What sounds do you hear? Does the house feel different? Do *you* feel different? Morning meditations can sometimes be "easier" because the day has yet to intrude on your experience, and your busy, chattering mind may still be a bit sleepy. Experiment with early morning practice and what it feels like for you.

SET YOUR *Intention*

As you begin your day, set an intention. Your intention is not your to-do list, it's your guidance for how you want to be in the world today. How do you want to feel? How do you want to show up today? Some of the mantras in this chapter might be your intentions for the day, and are meant for when you want to focus on just one aspect of mindfulness practice for a day.

MANTRA

I WELCOME TODAY.

"*Today* I WILL PRACTICE *Curiosity*"

Today I will look at the world with interest and curiosity. Instead of bringing my preconceived ideas and stories to the world, I will meet the world with a beginner's mind. I will be open to what unfolds, and approach my day with an eager inquisitiveness.

"*Today* I WILL PRACTICE *Friendship*"

Today I will reach out to a friend. I will listen to her stories and share mine. I will offer support and encouragement. I will nurture the relationships and connections that are important to me.

"*Today* I WILL PRACTICE *Tenderness*"

Today I will bring tenderness to all that I do. If today feels hard, I'll be soft and gentle with myself. I'll show compassion and warmth to others. I will practice tenderness with my voice, my body, and my thoughts.

"*Today* I WILL PRACTICE *Pride*"

Today I will take pride in the things I do for others, for myself, and for my world. I will honor myself for my hard work and all that I accomplish.

"*Today* I WILL PRACTICE *Hope*"

Today I will practice optimism. I will see the good wherever I can, and I will trust that even as difficult as things may be, there is always room for hope. I am strong and capable, and hopeful for the future.

Morning Coffee MEDITATION

Make some time today to truly savor the first few sips of your morning coffee or tea, instead of pouring a hot cup and then letting it get cold as you attend to more pressing concerns. Allow yourself a few moments to feel the warmth of the beverage where your hands make contact with the cup. Take a deep breath and inhale the rich aroma. Drink slowly and really taste the flavor of your morning libation. Notice the sensations in your throat and belly as you swallow. Perhaps even spend a silent moment in gratitude for caffeine and all it will help you do today.

WHAT IS YOUR *Morning Story?*

We're always telling stories, and you probably have a story about mornings. You might tell yourself that mornings are chaotic and stressful. While you certainly don't know how any one morning will actually turn out, see if you can approach your morning routine with a blank slate. Assuming the morning will be a disaster can sometimes make it so, as we end up filtering everything through our dim-colored glasses. Try welcoming the morning as a new experience, and even if things don't go the way you planned, you'll at least feel a lot calmer as it happens.

"*Today* I WILL PRACTICE *Authenticity*"

Today I will be myself. Today I will give voice to my needs and my feelings, even if it's only to myself. I will not try to hide or cover up; I will be authentically me.

"*Today* I WILL PRACTICE *Appreciation*"

Today I will notice all that I can be thankful for. I will appreciate even the littlest of joys, and I will be grateful for the opportunities to learn from difficult moments. I will express my gratitude for others, and honor the qualities I appreciate in myself.

"*Today* I WILL PRACTICE *Enthusiasm*"

Today I will bring eagerness. I will approach everything I do as if it were the most important thing to be doing (for in many ways, it is). I will bring energy and excitement and enthusiasm to my day, and I will notice how it feels to see each moment as worthy of intense interest and commitment.

MORNING *Body Scan*

In whatever posture is comfortable (lying down, sitting in a chair), take a deep breath and bring your attention to your lower body (legs and feet). Just notice the sensations that are present, if any, and take a moment to set an intention for how you want to move in the world today—do you want to slow down, or will you need to be a bit speedier and more efficient today? Bring your awareness to your torso, noticing the sensations in your chest and belly. With your next breath, set an intention for how you want to feel today—energetic, restful, joyful, peaceful, or something else? Then gently bring your attention to your arms and hands, and set an intention for how you will be with loved ones today, imagining them in your embrace. Finally, bring your awareness to your neck and face and head, and set an intention for how you will be present today. Take a few more deep breaths, and begin your day.

MORNING *Yoga*

Cats and dogs always stretch when they first get up, and we probably should, too. You can do some simple yoga as part of your morning practice—stand with your feet hip distance apart and stretch your arms up above your head (a lovely posture to welcome a new day). Get down on your hands and knees and gently round your back upward as you tuck your chin to your chest, and then drop your belly toward the floor as you lift your chin and your chest. This is more about moving and stretching your body in a way that feels good and nurturing than it is about getting a posture right. Listen to what your body needs.

"*Today* I WILL PRACTICE *Understanding*"

Today I will listen with the intent to understand. I won't get caught up in thinking about what I'm going to say or do, or how I'm going to fix a problem. I will listen to others and seek to know and comprehend their experience.

"*Today* I WILL PRACTICE *Empathy*"

Today I will do my best to see the world from other perspectives. I will bring compassion and understanding to others' problems, no matter how trivial they may seem. I will seek understanding and practice empathy.

"*Today* I WILL PRACTICE *Self-Compassion*"

Today I will speak kindly to myself. When things are difficult, I will take care of my needs without guilt. I will remember that the things that are hard for me are hard for everyone. I will offer love to myself without reservation or qualification.

"*Today* I WILL PRACTICE *Acceptance*"

Today I will accept. I will allow my thoughts, my feelings, and my experiences to be as they are. I will know that I am enough, just as I am right now.

CHECK IN WITH *Your Nervous System*

Before you move into your day, check in with your nervous system. Do you feel calm and stable? Or is your heart racing and your breath shallow? We are social animals, and the state of our nervous system impacts the nervous systems of those around us. If you feel agitated, take a few deep breaths, focusing on really allowing the belly to expand on the inhale, and then engaging the diaphragm on the exhale as you squeeze the air out of your lungs (you'll feel a sensation like you're trying to bring your belly button to your spine). Continue with a few deep breaths until you can feel your system begin to stabilize. This will allow you to share your calm, peaceful state with others as they begin their day.

MANTRA

TODAY IS THE MOST IMPORTANT DAY.

"*Today* I WILL PRACTICE *Creativity*"

Today I will seek out opportunities to create—I will color or paint or dance or sing or write or sew. I will practice discovery and innovation.

"*Today* I WILL PRACTICE *Movement*"

Today I will move with intention and awareness. I will be fully in my body, noticing my internal sensations as well as my body's interactions with the world. I will move in ways that feel good and nurturing and healthy for my body.

"*Today* I WILL PRACTICE *Contentment*"

Today I will not strive. Today I will not get caught in wanting. Today I will practice being okay with what I have, who I am, and who my loved ones are. Today I will be content.

HOLD YOUR *Intentions* LIGHTLY

You probably have a lot of things you want to get done today, and ways that you want to be today. Honor those intentions for your day, but hold them lightly. The world is not aware of your agenda, and your day may have other plans for you. Celebrate the things you accomplish, and greet the wrinkles and curveballs and unexpected roadblocks with as much patience and presence and compassion as you can. You may have set the intention to tackle a long to-do list today, but then the boiler broke down and you had wait in for the plumber. Allow your intention to shift as the events of your day unfold. Intentions should create a general direction and tone for your day, not dictate the precise path you must follow.

A MINDFUL SHOWER

Going to the spa is out of the question most days, but can you be completely present when you shower or take a bath? Enjoy the sensation of warm water on your skin, savor the scent of a favorite body wash, pay attention to the soothing sounds of running water. Instead of letting your mind wander to your to-do list, or running through your day in your head, just let your shower be a time to wash, and to care for yourself.

"*Today* I WILL PRACTICE *Quiet*"

Today I will welcome quiet and stillness. I will not try to fill silences that do not need filling, and I will make time for moments of peace and calm.

Morning MANTRA

Today I will be present.

Today I will pause before responding.

Today I will hold myself and others with compassion.

Today I will welcome my experiences, and try to meet each moment without resistance.

Today I will do my best, and be kind to myself when I know I could have done better.

Today I will be present.

"I'll Handle WHAT TODAY Brings"

When we get upset because things don't go according to our plan, it's often because we weren't aware of our plan in the first place, and we didn't recognize that we had an assumption that things would go our way. Notice what you're expecting today, so you can skillfully meet the moments that don't deliver. Repeat the mantra "I'll Handle What Today Brings."

MANTRA

TODAY I WILL BE PRESENT.

Breakfast MEDITATION

If you tend to skip breakfast, see if you can take a few moments to eat something healthy this morning, perhaps some yogurt or a piece of fruit, or peanut butter and banana on toast. If you can, try to really taste and enjoy the food, instead of eating on-the-go. Even if you only get three bites in silence, savor each one and allow eating breakfast to be a truly nourishing, if brief, experience.

"*Today* I WILL PRACTICE *Rest*"

Today I will rest. I will allow myself to nap, and I will claim renewal when I need it.

Morning Walk

If possible, make time for a walk as part of your morning routine. Take your time to be mindful of your surroundings—pay attention to the sights and sounds of the morning, such as the sun rising, birds singing, and traffic buzzing.

"*Today* I WILL PRACTICE *Trust*"

Today I will trust that I know just what I need, and just what my loved ones need. I will trust that I have, within me, all the wisdom and peace and stillness and love that I need.

EMBRACE *Today*

Today will unfold in its *own* special way. It's not predetermined, but it's also not fully up to you. Show up with presence, pause before acting, and engage with today the best way you know how.

Morning COMMUTE

If your morning routine involves any sort of commuting, it may sometimes be the most stressful part of your day. It can help to remind yourself that the commute is a short part of your day, and by the time you get home, the stressors of the morning are often long forgotten. Take a deep breath and focus on this moment, instead of letting your thoughts drift to "This *always* happens!" or "Tomorrow will be *exactly* like this, too." If you notice the same stressors each morning, see if you can make some changes, such as taking a different route or finding some stress relief by downloading meditations or relaxing music to listen to during your commute.

"*Today* I WILL PRACTICE *Wonder*"

Today I will welcome delight and surprise. I'll do my best to bring my attention to the little things I often overlook. I'll approach my day with a sense of enchantment and fascination and wonder.

MANTRA

TODAY IS A CHANCE TO START AGAIN.

DOES *Today's* TO-DO LIST *Include You*?

You may start your morning by running through your to-do list ... and you may discover you are not on it at all. You've met all your loved ones' needs and done what you need to for work ... but where are *you*? Like many people, you may get to the end of the day and have forgotten to take care of yourself. Take a moment to be mindful of your needs today (do you need to book a haircut? Can you make it to yoga class?) and see if you can put yourself on the to-do list.

CHAPTER 3

Sustain

MINDFULNESS THROUGHOUT THE DAY

Mindfulness is both a formal practice, and something we cultivate throughout the day. Mindfulness teacher Jon Kabat-Zinn likes to ask, "When does the meditation end?" Just because we've gotten up from our cushion doesn't mean we fall back into our regular mode of distraction and over-reaction. Use the practices in this chapter to sustain your mindfulness practice over the course of your day.

THE *Best Time of Day For* MEDITATION

The best time of day for meditation is the time of day when *you* will meditate—i.e. it is different for everyone. I prefer early morning, because the house is quiet, and I like knowing that the first thing I do in the day is just for me. But you need to find the time that will work for you. When are you most alert and least likely to get interrupted? It's helpful to pick a time that's relatively consistent, as this will help you keep your habit going. If morning doesn't work for you, see if you can practice during your lunchtime or before bed.

COME *Home* TO YOURSELF

No matter how far you travel and all the places you go throughout your day, you can come home to yourself at any time. Take a deep breath and bring your mind and body into the same place. Gently touching or lightly tapping your arms, legs, face, or shoulders can help you awaken the body, orient you to your environment, and create a moment of embodied presence.

Simplify

See if you can do one thing each day to simplify your life. Organize a drawer in the kitchen, cancel an appointment that's not necessary, or finally get all those apps on your phone into folders. It's amazing how creating space in our day and in our physical environment can help us feel more spacious and open.

WHAT IS MY *Motivation*?

Try to get into the habit of checking in with your motivation for the actions you take. Every move has an intention behind it, whether we are aware of it or not. Is your question "What should we do today?" an invitation for everyone to share their input, or an attempt to steer them to *your* agenda? Today, practice noticing the brief moments before you act. Investigate what has prompted your desire to act, what thoughts you're having about what the outcome will be, and whether the action you are about to take is one that is necessary and helpful in that moment. You might be surprised by how many times you act without thinking, or how some behaviors may be prompted by unskillful motivations. This isn't about judging or criticizing yourself. Think of it as gathering data to help you cultivate the insight that will help you act the way you want to in the world.

Mindful EXERCISE

Make your workouts mindful. Ditch the headphones and turn off the TV, and focus your attention on your amazing body and your powerful muscles and all the incredible things you can do with them. Make your exercise routine a true mind-body practice.

DROP *In*

At any moment of your day, you can "drop in": drop in to your body and notice what you are feeling. Notice your feet on the floor. Notice where you are and what you are doing. Just drop in to presence.

DRIVING *Meditation*

You would think we'd always be paying attention while driving, but in fact we are usually on auto-pilot. Today, try to be more mindful when you drive. Pay close attention not just to the road in front of you, but notice all that your body does as you drive—the pressure of your foot on the gas, the movement of your hands on the steering wheel. When you hit a red light, just sit at the red light. Notice if there's any restlessness. Turn off the radio and just notice what it's like to drive through your part of the world, truly aware of the things you often just, well, drive by.

Change IT UP

We are creatures of habit—every day we might eat the same breakfast, drive the same way to work, park in the same spot, and walk the same route with the dogs. It's not that habits are bad (indeed, having some things on auto-pilot frees up space in our head for more complicated activities). But habits can prevent us from engaging with our life with awareness. Today, see if you can change up a habit—brush your teeth with the opposite hand, sit in a different spot in your meeting, walk a different way to the park. See what you notice when you're not on auto-pilot.

Breathe BEFORE YOU SPEAK

For today, try taking a full breath with awareness before you speak. It doesn't need to be an obvious, deep yogic breath; it's simply a way for you to bring yourself completely into this moment before you speak and engage with another person. It allows you to be completely present in your conversation, and supports meaningful communication and understanding.

JUST *Hug*

When we give and receive hugs, our body releases oxytocin, a hormone that promotes bonding and trust. This makes us feel good and relaxed. So give your loved ones a hug, or even give yourself a hug! (Your neurons don't know it's you, so you'll still get a juicy dose of happy hormones if the hug comes from you.)

MINDFUL *Reminders*

Create small reminders to cue you to check in with your attention throughout the day. You could place stickers or dots in places you'll see them every day—on the refrigerator or on your computer. You could also make your cue a particular behavior that you do many times during the day—walking through a doorway, picking up your phone, turning off a light. When you see or "activate" your mindful reminder, just pause for a moment, and check in: What are you doing? Where's your attention? How do you feel? Is there anything you need?

A DAY OF *Kindness*

Make today a day of kindness. Write a note of gratitude to your partner or a good friend, or write down all the things you appreciate about yourself. See if you can offer kindness to strangers, too—a smile, a door held open, a sincere compliment ... no act is too small! Notice what it feels like to approach your day with kindness.

Waiting IN LINE MEDITATION

Today, pay attention to what you do when you're waiting in line—is there an urge to distract yourself with your phone? See what happens if you decide to be completely present with the experience of waiting in line. What if you engaged the cashier in conversation or simply allowed yourself to pause and breathe?

Mindful CLEANING

The repetitive movements of cleaning your home can be a soothing meditation if you choose to make them so. As you tidy up today, bring your awareness to the movements of your body. Notice the sights and smells and sounds around you. Take a moment to express gratitude for the spaces and objects you are cleaning. Your daily chores can be drudgery—or you can make them a special practice in caring for your home and protecting those who live in it with you. The choice is yours.

MANTRA

I WILL MOVE THROUGH MY DAY WITH AWARENESS AND ATTENTION.

A Day OF NO COMPLAINING

Challenge yourself to an entire day of not complaining. Notice when the tendency arises to say what you don't like about something, or state your wish that things were other than they are. Is there a different way you can approach the situation? Can you say something positive or constructive instead? This doesn't mean you have to go through your day saying "Everything is awesome!" It's simply an invitation to notice how perseverating on the things we don't like can impact our day, and to experiment with a different way of being.

Slow DOWN

See if there is a part of your day that you can deliberately slow down. It might be walking at a more regular pace rather than speed walking to the store or to your place of work or doing an everyday task more slowly and mindfully. You don't need to go obnoxiously slow—try to go about 70 percent of your regular speed. What does it feel like to slow down? If you're usually really fast (like most of us are), you might discover that it's actually quite normal and acceptable, and in fact a bit pleasanter, to move slightly less forcefully through the world. (If you find you prefer hurried movement, that's okay too. The point is to be mindful of what you do, no matter what your pace.)

BE *Still*

For one whole minute today, just be still. No movement, no noise. Just be still.

I AM TOO DISTRACTED *To Be Mindful*

But what if you saw all those distractions as *part of the practice?* What if you brought your mindful awareness to distraction? How do you feel in your body when interruptions occur? What thoughts arise? What *involuntary* responses do you typically enact (sighing, gritting your teeth, clenching your fists)? What *voluntary* responses emerge (complaining, getting upset, allowing)? In mindfulness, a distraction is not an obstacle to practice—it is the practice. We work with whatever arises.

BE *Creative*

Make time today for something that's creative or artistic. Turn on some music and dance, write in a journal, work on a scrapbook, arrange some flowers, do some baking, or something else that gets your creative juices flowing! When we focus our attention on a creative task, we often enter a state of meditative absorption called "flow," which the research tells us is a very pleasurable state, and one that frees the mind to think in new ways.

ARE YOU *Pounding* THE PAVEMENT?

I mean that question literally—when you walk around during the day, do you pound the pavement, slamming your feet into the ground instead of lightly stepping on the earth? You can cause yourself all sorts of aches and pains when you walk with heavy legs and feet, which sends a jarring impact through your spine. Can you try walking softly today, imagining that your feet and legs are weightless as you bring them to the ground?

ONE *Mindful* ACTIVITY

Choose one activity today that you will do with complete presence and attention. Try to pick something that you often do mind-*less*-ly, such as cooking, walking to your desk at work, or doing a household chore. Pay attention to the movements of your body, your internal sensations, and the sounds and sights and smells around you. Notice what it's like to be completely present in very ordinary moments.

HOW DO YOU *Avoid*?

We all have our particular go-to strategies for avoiding unpleasant emotions or discomfort. Today, see if you can bring your attention to the ways you might distract yourself from your own experience—it might be something obvious like grabbing your phone or watching television, or it might be more subtle, like blaming others, getting angry, or explaining things away ("I'm just tired . . ."). When you notice these strategies, try to stay mindfully with your difficult experience, even if just for a few seconds. As you start to become more aware of your avoidance practices, you can ask yourself, "Am I doing this as a way to escape? Can I stay with this difficult moment instead?" You may discover that the discomfort is not as unbearable as it seems.

Standing MEDITATION

You don't always have to find time to sit or lie down to meditate. Try this standing meditation (a great time is when you're waiting in line at the store). As you stand, notice your feet grounding into the floor. Put down baskets or bags and slowly shift your weight from side to side, feeling the earth support you. Gently bend your knees, and tuck your pelvis in to reduce strain on your back. Roll your shoulders up and back and allow your arms to hang effortlessly at your side.

TWO-MINUTE *Self-Care*

Self-care doesn't have to be extensive or expensive. There are lots of things you can do in just 5 minutes (or less) that can nourish you and give you some refueling during your day. If you have just 2 minutes, you can:

- Drink a full glass of water.
- Step outside and take some deep breaths.
- Close your eyes and breathe.
- Call or text a friend.
- Listen to your favorite song.
- Do a few gentle yoga stretches or poses.

Who's Driving?

Throughout your day, ask yourself, "Who's driving?" Are you present and in control, making decisions with awareness and intention? Or has your auto-pilot taken over, leading you to make careless mistakes or be driven by habitual reactions? When you notice your inner chauffer has taken the wheel on a route she's not really equipped for, see if you can get yourself back in the driver's seat.

NOT NOW

One of my teachers says that "not now" is always an acceptable response to a difficult moment. We don't always have the emotional bandwith to process an intense experience, or we may not be in the right place for deep self-exploration. In those moments, you can note what is arising and say, "Not now." You're not suppressing your experience; you're recognizing it for what it is, and wisely intuiting that now is not the right time. If it's a BIG something that's arising, you can be pretty sure it will be back another time for you to work with it. So breathe, allow the experience to be as it is, and then reflect on the difficult moment when you have the time and space to do so.

Walking MEDITATION

Most of us walk simply as a means to an end—we have somewhere we need to be. Can you make walking an intentional activity today? As you walk, observe how your body moves and feels. Can you sense how your body moves as you take each step? Can you feel all the different muscles that engage in so many different ways as you do this complicated activity with ease every single day? Notice the sensations of placing your feet on the ground, attend to your breath and your heart rate, and take a look at the world (or gym) around you. Meditation doesn't always have to happen on your cushion. You can be mindful as you walk (and run and skip and tiptoe) through your day.

As If

In *The Power of Now*, author and spiritual teacher Eckhart Tolle writes, "Whatever the present moment contains, accept it as if you had chosen it." Can you bring this attitude to your day today? Can you greet every moment as if it were exactly as you would have designed it?

CHEST Openers

Often, we aren't even aware of the tension in our upper body until we collapse into bed, achy and exhausted. Simple exercises throughout the day can help us release these tensions. Try standing up and stretching your arms behind you, clasping your hands together if you can. Lift your head and chest and pull your shoulders back. Do these several times a day when you need a quick stretch.

DON'T FIND TIME—*Make Time*

We often put time for ourselves pretty low on our list of priorities. It becomes something we do "when I find the time." If we want time to ourselves—to pause and breathe, to take a hot shower, or to savor a cup of coffee—we need to make the time. Pay attention to how you use your time today. Do you notice that there are periods of "wasted" time that could be used for nourishing self-care? Are there commitments that you can drop from your routine? See if you can make time in your day that's just for you.

Nurture YOUR BODY

Your ability to handle stressors and summon the energy to do all that you need to do today depends on how you treat your body—what you eat, how you move, and when you sleep. Be mindful of what you eat, seeing if you can opt for something healthy (bonus points if it has protein), instead of mindlessly snacking on sugary foods that don't fuel your body. Find opportunities to move your body, even if it's not "exercise"—walk to the store, or park at the far end of the parking lot. Take the stairs instead of the elevator, go for a short walk at lunch, or try to make time for a quick cardio workout.

PHONE *Awareness*

Most of us spend too much time on our phones and, while you don't need to ditch your phone completely, you can be more mindful of what you're using it for and how it makes you feel. When you put down your phone, notice how you feel. Did you just laugh at a goofy cat video and now you feel relaxed and happy? Great! Did you just check Instagram and now you feel completely miserable and totally inferior after seeing the perfect-looking meals and art projects and home repairs everyone else is doing? Hmmm … This isn't about judging yourself for being on your phone, but simply taking in the information your body is giving you about how the way you spend your time impacts how you feel.

MANTRA

I CAN MAKE ANY MOMENT A MINDFUL MOMENT.

CHAPTER 4

Support

MINDFULNESS FOR DIFFICULT MOMENTS

The meditations in the previous chapters are the practice for the stuff we need to deal with here: how to keep our cool when people start pushing buttons we didn't even know we had. When these difficult moments arise, you have a choice: how are you going to be with them? Are you going to fight the difficulty? Are you going to kick and scream at it? Are you going to wish it away? Or are you going to allow it, get curious about it, and then see what happens in the next moment? The meditations and practices in this chapter will help you in doing the latter, so you can meet the hard parts of your day with greater ease.

Under THE SEA

It can help to think of a rough moment of your day as a stormy sea: the violent waves, heavy rain, and screaming thunder capture and almost overwhelm your attention. But if you were to dip below the surface, and peer down a little bit, you'd see that the bottom of the sea is perfectly cool and still. When the storms of your day assault the sense receptors at the top of your body, flooding your eyes and ears and the space between with sound and fury, see if you can drop down into your body, sensing your breath in your belly and your feet on the ground, and find some stillness under the sea.

"I Am Enough"

You are enough. Your presence, your worries, your love, your mistakes, your hugs, your sorrys, your smiles, your tears, your kisses, your failures, your joy ... it's all enough. You don't need to be anyone or anything but you. Tell yourself, "I am enough."

I Can DO THIS

As hard as things get during your day, remind yourself, "I can do this." You've done hard things before. Know that whatever it is you are facing, you already have everything you need to handle it. You have your presence, your attention, and your breath. You've got this. Repeat the mantra "I Can Do This."

Begin AGAIN

Every moment of every day is a chance to make a fresh start. Each moment is an opportunity to pause, to apologize, to help, to listen. Each moment is an invitation to revisit your intentions and begin again.

Overwhelm

Mindfulness teacher Shinzen Young says that overwhelm is a "loss of sensory discrimination"—we become so flooded with sensations that we cannot separate or distinguish them. With mindful awareness, we cultivate the ability to break down our emotions into distinct sensory events. When you feel overwhelmed today, see if you can stop and identify the component parts of your experience. What bodily sensations are present? What's happening in your mind? Seeing the moment as a composition of various sensations, thoughts, memories, and judgments makes it much more manageable than a vague, but powerful, feeling of "overwhelm."

MANTRA

MY PRESENCE IS ENOUGH.

Story TIME

In her book *Rising Strong*, researcher Brené Brown suggests that we approach a difficult moment with, "The story I'm telling myself right now is …" Sometimes, we're telling the story of the hardworking parent whose children are ungrateful and whose spouse is unhelpful, and sometimes we're telling a story about our co-workers judging us and thinking we're doing a terrible job. It's helpful to take a look at the stories you are telling yourself throughout the day. Are they true? Are they helpful? If those stories weren't there, what would be?

WHAT DO I *Need*?

If you're someone who often puts everyone else's needs ahead of your own, it's difficult even to think to ask, "What do I need?" Take a moment today to consider your needs: Do you need more sleep? Do you need more help at home or at work? Do you need 10 minutes to yourself? Do you need to take five deep breaths? Whatever it is you need, don't be afraid to name it and claim it.

If Only …

How often during the day do our thoughts turn to "If only …"? "If only I weren't so tired," "If only I had more money." Well, things are only as they are … and we add to our suffering when we keep wishing they were somehow different. For today, pay attention to the times when you are hoping for something other than what is happening—when you are wishing a loved one were different, or you were different, or your house were different. You don't need to get upset with yourself for thinking this way (we all do it!)—just notice this common habit of our minds. When you notice these thoughts, pay attention to how they make you feel, and ask yourself, "Can I accept this moment, this house, this me, exactly as it is, right here and right now?"

WHAT DO I *Control*?

Sometimes you can take refuge in Reinhold Niebuhr's *Serenity Prayer*, which counsels us to change the things we can change, and to accept the things we cannot. If you've hit a tough moment, ask yourself, "What do I control?" There's a lot you do not control—the weather, traffic, illnesses, other people's behavior, to name just a few. But in every moment, there is at least something you can control—perhaps it's your response, your attitude, or simply your breath. Take a deep breath, and allow the things you don't control to be as they are. Take another deep breath, and engage in wise action toward the things you *do* control.

MANTRA

I CAN HANDLE THIS.

HELLO, ANXIETY

One of the most powerful mindfulness practices is to greet our emotions. The poet Rumi said we should invite our emotions into our lives as welcome guests. When I feel frustration or irritation or anxiety, I sometimes smile and say to myself (in a silent, though booming, inner voice), "Hello, Anxiety!" It sounds silly, but it works. Sometimes I'll say, "Thank you for coming by and reminding me of all the things I need to do, but I've got this." Today, try greeting your emotions by name. Thank them for the information they are providing you!

Don't Cry OVER SPILLED MILK

When milk has spilled onto the kitchen floor, what is needed of you? You need to clean up the milk. You can't go back in time and unspill the milk. You can't yell at the milk (well, you can … but let me know how that goes). What you can do is clean up the milk. You can clean up the milk with anger and resentment, or you can clean up the milk with presence and without judgment. You can clean up the milk and let your mind go wild with irritating thoughts of how many more times you'll be cleaning up today. Or you can clean up the milk with thoughts about cleaning up this milk from this floor right now. The choice is yours.

Feel YOUR *Feels*

Whatever you are feeling right now, truly *feel* it. Notice the sensations in your body—is there tightness or softness, warmth or coolness? Bring your attention to your thoughts, to any desires to take action, and see if you can identify what you are feeling. Research shows that suppressing emotions causes greater stress than experiencing them. And, as intense as it may be, an emotion usually lasts only about 90 seconds. Once the emotion has begun, you're on the ride, so see if you can stay with it, observe it, feel it, and watch it subside.

MANTRA

I DON'T LIKE THIS. BUT I CAN BE WITH IT.

"IT IS HARD RIGHT NOW *and that's Okay*"

When you have a rough day, simply say to yourself, "It's hard right now, and that's okay." Just acknowledging that things are tough will make you feel better. You can even ask, "What do I need to do to take care of myself during this challenging time?" Whatever you are experiencing is completely normal ... because it's what you are experiencing! You don't need to try to talk yourself out of how you are feeling. Simply say to yourself, "Sometimes it's hard, and that's okay."

DO NOT RESIST

When your day doesn't go according to plan, you have two choices: resist, or go with it. So often, our first instinct is to resist ("I don't want it to be this way," "I wanted this to happen instead.") But resisting what is happening—resisting the present moment—is exhausting, and it usually just makes things worse. When your day gets derailed, take a deep breath, and instead of fighting the present moment, see if you can soften into it. You don't have to like it, but it is here. Don't resist.

WORK FROM THE *Bottom* TO THE *Top*

When you're really stressed out, it can be hard to access the mental bandwidth to use strategies such as reframing a crisis into an opportunity or investigating the needs behind your emotions. So start at the bottom: breathe, move your body a bit, sit up a bit taller, and just focus on being present with your breath. Pay attention to your body as you begin to activate your natural calming response (you can use the practices from Chapter 1 to do this).

Once you've soothed your body's stress response and brought your thinking back online, you can use your go-to cognitive strategies to meet your stress. You can reflect on the times in the past when you've handled something similar, you can practice reframing (see page 111), consider what you can learn from this moment (see page 121), or find meaning in a difficult situation (see page 122).

DEALING WITH STRESS

"Top Down" Practices

MEANING:
Is there something I can learn from this?

REFRAME:
Is there another way to look at this?

MEMORY:
How have I dealt with this in the past?

"Bottom Up" Practices

BREATHE:
Breathe from the belly.
Lengthen the exhale.

EMBODY:
Sit up.
Move.
Exercise.

Everyone's HARD IS HARD

It's tempting to try to talk yourself out of feeling upset when there are people who are in much worse situations than you are all over the globe. But you know what? *Everyone's hard is hard.* If it's hard for you, then it's hard. You needn't feel guilty for acknowledging your own pain and difficulty; in fact, that's how you will strengthen yourself so that you may help others.

Reframing

Psychologists tell us that many of our problems can become less overwhelming if we can reframe them, for there are many vantage points from which a situation can be viewed. When you're stuck in resentment or worry or frustration, ask yourself if you can put this scenario in a different frame. Is this person willful and stubborn, or is he passionate and confident? Is this another half hour of drudgery doing chores, or an opportunity to look after your home environment and living space? Is this yet another week at work or an opportunity to use your skills, earn money, and make a contribution? The choice is yours.

MANTRA

I DESERVE CARE AND EMPATHY.

Forgiveness MEDITATION

If you are struggling with your feelings of being hurt by someone, see if you can practice a silent forgiveness meditation. Bring to mind the person you want or need to forgive—it may be a relative, a friend, a co-worker, or even yourself. Notice any negative judgments or thoughts that arise. Silently say to this person, "I forgive you. If you could have done better, in that moment, you would have." Forgiving someone doesn't mean you are condoning what they did or releasing them from the consequences of their action. It means you are releasing *yourself* from resentment and anger. Forgiveness can be a difficult practice, and it may help to repeat this exercise a few times.

MANTRA

I DON'T NEED TO BE PERFECT.

I CANNOT DO IT ALL AT ONCE

I'll be honest, I've rebelled against this mantra many times, but each time I do, I realize its frustrating truth: we simply cannot do it all, all at the same time. If I divide my limited energy among *all the things* I want to do, I end up with a complicated equation that will never balance. I've learned there are times when I need to put one of my passions on hold, times when I have to lean in and do something difficult, and times when space opens up that's just for me. I've learned it's more about bringing my all to all that I do, and trusting that I can do it all, just not all at once. So when you're juggling too many things, gently remind yourself, "I Can't Do It All At Once."

Some Days ARE JUST NOT HAPPY DAYS

Mindfulness is not going to make us happy all the time (nor, really, would we want it to). Some days, honestly, are just miserable—our loved ones are cranky, we're cranky, and nothing turns out as we expected. That's just how some days are. Please don't put pressure on yourself to be smiling and happy every day. If it's a hard day, just sit with your hard day. It's okay, and it won't last.

HOW DO YOU SPEAK TO YOURSELF?

Do you speak to yourself in ways you would never permit another person to speak to you? Your self-talk matters: negative self-talk can trigger your stress response, and it just makes you feel miserable. For today, pay attention to your inner voice. Are you speaking to yourself as you would a dear friend? Are you treating yourself with understanding and compassion? If you notice that you're being overly critical, see if you can offer yourself some kindness instead.

THIS, TOO, SHALL *Pass*

My mother said this to me many times when I was going through difficult times. It helped me remember that no emotion, phase, or pain lasts forever. Sometimes the ever-changing and shifting nature of the world is a challenge, and sometimes we can take comfort in the impermanent nature of our experience.

PEACE AND STILLNESS ARE ALWAYS AVAILABLE

No matter what is happening in your day, peace and stillness are always only a breath (or five!) away. You'd be amazed at how soothing just 10 seconds of being fully aware of your breathing can be. If you notice yourself becoming agitated, remind yourself that *peace can always be found within you*. You have everything you need. Always.

ALL THE *Terrible* THINGS

Mark Twain supposedly once quipped, "I've been through a lot of terrible things in my life, some of which actually happened." Can you notice the times when you allow yourself to get completely caught up in the drama and trauma of an event that is not actually happening? When you catch yourself doing this, see if you can remember Twain's mocking words, and remind yourself to focus on what is *actually* happening.

"I AM NOT MY *Anger*"

When we say, "I am angry," it's almost as if we become anger itself; we completely identify with this emotion and it takes over our entire experience. With mindfulness, we try to see an emotion as something that arises within us; we notice that anger is present, not that we "are" angry. When a difficult emotion arises today, tell yourself, "I am not this emotion." You are not sadness, or fear, or jealousy, or any other single component of your experience—you contain multitudes! You are the awareness that holds all that is happening within you, including your emotional experiences. See if you can observe the emotion objectively, rather than identifying with it. Taking this more detached stance toward emotions can help you respond more skillfully in a difficult moment.

EVERYDAY SELF-CARE

Self-care is as important a part of our day as brushing our teeth and eating healthy food. Self-care isn't just adding in a few side dishes of massages and pedicures—it's an essential ingredient that must be baked into our days. Find the things you can do every day that nourish you—a brief walk outside, a warm cup of tea, a good book before bed, a few minutes of meditation—and make them an integral part of your daily routine.

MANTRA

I ACCEPT.

SHUN THE "*Shoulds*"

One word we can get stuck on is "should": I *should* be doing this, I *should* be doing that. With all the pressure to multitask, it's easy to convince yourself that you *should* be doing something *more* than what you're doing right now. Remind yourself that you are most effective when you are doing one thing at a time. If it helps, you can keep a "should list" nearby so you can jot down the activities that must be attended to later; then you can return your attention to the present moment and the task at hand.

WATCH OUT FOR THE "*Always*"

The word "always" tends to creep into our mental chatter in difficult moments. "They *always* act this way!" "He's *always* late." Today, watch out for "always." It's a seductive mind-trap that can fuel and intensify your anger. But "always" is rarely right! When "always" enters your thoughts today, take a moment to ask, "Really? *Always*?"

HOW DO YOU *Handle* STRESS?

We all have different ways of managing stress. For the next few days, keep track of the things you do when you get stressed out or overwhelmed—write down the little responses, such as sighing or gritting your teeth, as well as the more time-consuming ones, such as reaching for your phone, exercising, napping, or eating junk food. After a few days, consider your list and think about which of your stress responses are working for you, and which ones aren't. Which ones are soothing or energizing, and which ones are agitating or draining? Which ones do you need more of? Are there any that you need less of?

This TOO

When you hit a difficult moment, see if you can welcome it with, "This, too." This, too, is part of your experience. This, too, is something that can be held in your gentle awareness. This, too, may not be pleasant, but you can be with it.

Insight MEDITATION

Mindfulness meditation is sometimes called "insight meditation," which is a perfect description of the practice: we pay attention in order to cultivate insight and wisdom. Through carefully attending to your experience, you may discover that you hit the same problems every week. Think of this as an invitation to consider possible solutions. Can you take a different route to work? Can you find a more effective way to communicate with your boss? Can you and your partner synchronize your diaries more effectively? When you start to see all your experiences as data, you can figure out what's working, what's NOT working, and find new solutions.

MANTRA

I WILL CHOOSE TO SEE IT THIS WAY INSTEAD.

MEANING

Psychiatrist and Holocaust survivor Viktor Frankl has said that "suffering ceases to be suffering at the moment it finds a meaning." When things are hard, can you find the meaning? Is there a lesson to be learned, a new direction to be explored? The meaning of a particularly difficult time in your life may not be readily apparent, but you can probably think of harrowing times in your past that helped shape you into who you are today. Can you trust that if the meaning is not discernible right now, it will be some day?

A LOVING KINDNESS MEDITATION FOR YOU

Take a deep breath and place your hand on your heart. Imagine sending yourself as much love and acceptance as you can, and silently repeat the following phrases to yourself:

May I be happy.
May I be healthy.
May I be safe.
May I be peaceful.
May I be present.
May I be accepting.
May I be kind to myself.
May I be patient.
May I be curious.
May I be engaged.
May I be hopeful.
May I be loved.
May I be loving.
May I be joyful.
May I be full of life.

A *Balanced* APPROACH TO BALANCE

We often talk about wanting to "find balance," as if it were a solid thing we must discover or a destination where we must arrive. But it's much more helpful to think of balance as a dance. In fact, in ballet, a balance is a move performed by gently shifting your weight from one foot to the other, and I think that's a healthier way to approach balance. Sometimes you lean into your work, sometimes you lean harder into family time, but you're rarely completely still, holding everything up all at once in some complicated pose. Balance is not something we achieve; it's something we do. It's a dance.

"Thanks, but I've got this"

This is my favorite mantra for when my inner critic likes to offer up words such as, "You're a terrible mother" or "You are never going to be any good at this." I simply say, "Thanks for the input. I know you're just doing the whole worrying thing that your part of the brain is supposed to be doing. But I've GOT this."

NURTURE YOUR *Friendships*

While Facebook and text messages offer great ways to stay in digital touch with our friends, there's no substitute for old-fashioned analog communication. Instead of texting back and forth, can you give your friend a call and chat for a few minutes? Could you even find some time to meet for coffee?

YOU GET *To Choose*

In any given moment, you can choose your:

- Attitude
- Words
- Actions

It's an incredible power. Choose joyfully, with presence and wisdom.

MANTRA

HOW CAN I BE KIND TO MYSELF TODAY?

CHAPTER 5

Savor

MINDFUL APPRECIATION

Our brains have what psychologists call a "negativity bias," which means we pay more attention to negative events than positive ones. This serves an evolutionary purpose, because it means we're attentive to danger, but sadly it also means we miss out on a lot of the small, ordinary joys. In this chapter, you'll learn practices that will help you pay more attention to the good (which is really good for you), and how to savor the fleeting moments of beauty that life offers us.

Pay Attention TO THIS MOMENT

Since moments are so … momentary … we may think that any individual moment isn't all that important. But what's in a moment? A breath, a thought, a memory, a worry, a smile, a sneeze. A sip of water, a twinge in your knee, a bug on the wall, a breeze just outside, a dog barking, a car in the distance. The hum of the lights, a creak in the floor, the air conditioner kicking in, the buzzing of your phone. What's in a moment? Just everything.

Smile

Research shows that smiling makes you feel happier. Take a deep breath in, and on the exhale, bring your lips into a slight smile (think more "Mona Lisa" and less "say cheese!"). Hold your gentle smile for a few seconds, and notice how it feels.

MUSIC
Meditation

Put on some music you like and pay attention to how you feel as you listen. What do you notice in your body? What thoughts arise? Does the music make you feel calm, energized, or something else? Savor the power music has to awaken so many emotions, memories, thoughts, sensations, and experiences.

MANTRA

I WILL BE PRESENT FOR THIS SPECIAL AND PRECIOUS MOMENT.

TOTALLY *Awesome*

When we experience awe, we feel good. Awe is a sense of being part of something bigger than ourselves, or an experience of having to adjust and expand our thinking to accommodate unexpected information. We generally experience awe when we 1) are outdoors, or 2) witness unexpected kind acts. So take some time to step outside today and admire the big, beautiful world: the vast sky above your home and the steady trees in your yard. And when you see an act of kindness today, soak it in and experience the awesome.

WHEN WE *Cling* TO THE *Good*

With mindfulness, we come to realize that all of our difficult moments will ultimately pass. And that means our good moments will eventually come to an end, too. The secret to truly living and loving those moments is to not cling to them. Sometimes we hold those experiences so tightly, fearing they may never come again, that we almost crush them. We don't even really enjoy them because we're so worried that they'll end. They *will* end, as all moments do. When we don't frantically cling to the good, and relax into it instead, it expands and nourishes us.

Connect WITH NATURE

Our modern lives disconnect us from a basic part of our nature, which is connecting with nature! Get outside today and let your bare feet touch the earth, feel the wind on your face, take in the smell of the outdoors, and listen to the sounds of the world around you. In the summer months, you could even consider doing your daily mindfulness and meditation practice outdoors.

Safe PLACE

Where are the places in your body where you generally feel good and safe? Where do you *not* tend to carry a lot of emotion and tension? For most people, these safe places in the body are near the extremities—the hands, the knees, the feet. Our difficult emotions tend to be felt in the gut or the chest, so spend some time savoring the sensations in the parts of the body that feel safe.

THIS IS WHAT *Calm* FEELS LIKE

Today, bring special attention to the moments when you feel calm. It's easy to miss them because they're so, well, calm. When you notice that your body is at rest, your muscles are relaxed, and your heart rate and breathing are slow, simply note, "This is what calm feels like." Spend a few moments savoring— and remembering—the calm. Know that you can call upon this feeling of calm at any moment of your day.

Savor THE SWEET

We often overlook the small moments of goodness and sweetness in our midst (which is a good thing for our physical survival, but not so good for our mental health). Research shows that we need to spend about 20 seconds with a positive experience to make it "stick." Today, set an intention to savor the sweet. When someone gives you a hug, or makes you laugh, take a deep breath and be fully in that moment. Notice how it feels when you are happy and joyful. Savor the sweet.

MANTRA

I WILL FULLY EXPERIENCE THIS GOOD FEELING.

MAKE A *Happy List*

Make a list of the things that make you feel happy. What is it that brings you joy? What makes you feel safe? When do you feel a sense of *enough*, a sense of not-wanting? Post your list where you can see it—continue to add to it, allow it to inspire you, and, if it makes you happy, smile whenever you walk past it.

A *Mindful* JAR

Each day, take a small piece of paper and write down one experience you had of being mindful during the day (a time you were fully present, a moment you truly appreciated, a freak-out you managed to soothe with your breath). Put this paper in a Mindful Jar (a simple canning jar will work), and after a few weeks and months you'll have a lovely collection of savored moments.

One Word JOURNAL

Keep a small journal in which you write down ONE WORD each day. It could be a word to describe yourself and how you felt or something that sums up your entire day. Perhaps you could describe your busy day as "full," or simply note that the day was "exhilarating," "challenging," "overwhelming," or "exciting." After a few weeks and months, you'll have a vivid portrayal of how much your experience can vary from day to day.

MANTRA

I HAVE SO MUCH TO BE THANKFUL FOR.

Joy

Joy can be found in any moment of your day. Happiness is fleeting, and is often tied to specific circumstances, but joy is enduring. Joy can be about finding the space between wanting and not-wanting, between pushing and pulling. You can find joy in the simple rest between two deep breaths. Joy can be a peaceful acceptance of every moment.

Camera Roll MEDITATION

Take a few moments to scroll through the camera roll on your phone. Spend some time appreciating your loved ones, revisiting a happy memory, and marveling at how much of your beautiful life is captured (and how much is not captured) on this little device.

EXPAND YOUR *Worldview*

Seek out opportunities to expand your worldview and see things from a new perspective. Read a book, listen to a podcast, or watch a documentary on something that is unfamiliar to you. Savor the experience of learning something new.

COME *Alive*

What makes you feel *alive*? What do you do that truly energizes you, that awakens a sense of empowerment and vitality? It might be dancing, running, walking, cooking, crafting … anything that you experience with mind and body and leaves you feeling strong and invigorated. Whatever it is, make some time for it today.

Good Enough REASONS

In his book *Waking Up*, neuroscientist Sam Harris writes, "Most of us spend our time seeking happiness and security without acknowledging the underlying purpose of our search. Each of us is looking for a path back to the present: We are trying to find good enough reasons to be satisfied *now*." I love the line: "good enough reasons to be satisfied *now*." Life will never be perfect, so can you be satisfied? Can you look for the "good enough" today? Can you appreciate that "good enough" is pretty amazing?

Equanimity

I think equanimity is the most beautiful—and important—concept in mindfulness. "Equanimity" literally means "equal strength," but it's sometimes referred to as "non-interfering." With mindfulness, we have the strength to be in the middle of some pretty strong forces—love and hurt, joy and anger, beauty and boredom. We have the strength to meet our experience without clinging or pushing, without trying to make it anything other than what it is. It's a way of standing in the middle of everything with courageous power, not passive resignation. It's a dynamic way of being in the world with presence. It is absolutely life-changing to approach our daily experiences with equanimity.

MINDFUL *Journaling*

Journaling may be one of the best forms of therapy. It's a great way to connect with yourself and your emotions, and can help you understand what you feel and who you are. Spend a few moments each day writing. Don't worry about structure and grammar—this is just for you. You could even set a timer for 5 minutes and just free-write. Many writers have said that they don't really know what they think until they write it down. Journaling can be a powerful part of your mindfulness practice, as you become more familiar with your thoughts. You can use your journal as a place to "dump" your thoughts without having to return to them, or you can use it to reflect on your growth or to sort out your thoughts about a difficult situation.

Sing!

When you sing, you take a short inhalation, and then let the words out with a long exhalation. It's a musical form of belly breathing! Even if it's just in the shower, or by yourself in the car, channel your inner diva and belt out some tunes today.

Visual REST

Your eyes take in so much information and stimulation throughout the day—and they need a break. Take a minute to close your eyes and notice what it feels like to give your vision a rest.

NOTHING *Special* IS HAPPENING

Meditation can sometimes seem boring. But the beauty of meditation is that when nothing special is happening, something special *is* happening. You are breathing. You are alive. You are completely awake and present to your experience. That is incredibly special.

Today I WILL NOTICE

Set an intention to *notice* today. Perhaps you want to notice acts of generosity, things that are beautiful, kindly spoken words, or freely given smiles. When we intentionally look for things, we're much more likely to see them, and we can remind ourselves that goodness is always waiting to be discovered.

DO *Some* GOOD

Find a way to do some good in your part of the world—volunteer, donate items to a local charity, or clean up the neighborhood park. Enjoy the feeling of playing a part in your community.

MANTRA

I WILL LOOK FOR THE GOOD.

FEEL *Gratitude*

When something powerful or amazing happens, we often describe being "moved" or "touched": it's a *physical* experience. Spend some time today reflecting on the good things in your life that you are thankful for, and notice how it feels in the body when you cultivate joy and gratitude.

Flow

Psychologist Mihaly Csikszentmihalyi tells us that one of the most positive mental experiences we can have is a state of *flow*. We usually achieve flow when we're doing a challenging and enjoyable activity that matches, or is just above, our ability level, and we're doing it purely for the sake of the activity itself. We focus on our task with a single-pointed concentration, and things just … flow. What activities create a flow state for you? It might be reading, knitting, gardening, sewing, coloring, or any number of endeavors. Take some time to explore the things that allow you to flow, and then do them, frequently and joyfully.

YOU HAVE NEVER SEEN *Today*

Sure, you've seen Mondays, holidays, sunny days, rainy days, and laundry days before, but you've never seen today. Can you drop your expectations and stories about today? You may be just a few hours into today, but you've already decided "Today is *this*" or "Today is *that*." But you've never seen today. Can you keep your eyes—and mind—open?

Read A POEM

Read your favorite poem today. Read it out loud and notice the words that jump out at you. Pay attention to your body and how it feels as you read. Savor the power that someone else's words can have on your experience. (If you don't have a favorite poem, you can easily explore poetry online. Try reading Rumi's "The Guest House" or Portia Nelson's "Autobiography in Five Short Chapters" to get started.)

DAY *Dreaming*

You can't be 100 percent mindful and attentive 100 percent of the time … nor would you really want to be. Research shows that mind-wandering is actually good for us (provided we don't do it when we're driving or performing surgery). When the mind wanders, we often stumble upon solutions and creative ideas that our purpose-driven, thinking mind would never discover. Take a few quiet moments today just to let your mind wander, and see where it goes.

WHEN THE *Stars Align*

The good and ordinary moments can pass us by because they're just that—ordinary. But if today you happen to capture a moment when everyone is in a good mood and things feel harmonious and there's no crisis, stop and take it in. As far as I'm concerned, that's a "stars aligning" moment, and it is meant to be treasured and savored.

INVITE *Laughter*

What makes you laugh? Whatever it is, seek it out today. Watch silly cat videos, read a good book, watch your favorite comedy, tell jokes, or play a physical game such as charades. Laughing is probably the most fun way to breathe ... so get your silly on today and make that your mindfulness practice.

MANTRA

MAY I SEE THE BEAUTY IN EVERYTHING.

CHAPTER 6

Close of Day

EVENING PRACTICES

Today you had an invitation—to show up, to make mistakes, to make amends, and to pay attention. Tonight is a time to invite rest and reflection. It is a time to be compassionate with yourself for your mistakes, to commit to new intentions for tomorrow, and to nurture yourself with loving care and restorative sleep. In this chapter, you'll find practices for closing your day with presence, stillness, and love.

MANTRA

I DID MY BEST TODAY.

THE *Good*, THE *Difficult*, AND THE *Helpful*

Take time out at the end of the day to sit down and reflect on what was good today, what was hard today, and who you helped today (or who helped you). It's a lovely way to take a balanced look at the day, and to remind ourselves about how we want to interact with others.

Tomorrow I WILL DO BETTER

We all have rough days. We all have days when we yell, when we lose it, when we're not present. When you have one of those days, take a deep breath. Place your hand on your heart and remind yourself that you did the best you could with the resources (time, energy, sanity) that you had today. On the in-breath, send yourself some kindness and compassion. On the out-breath, remember that tomorrow is a chance to begin again. Tomorrow, you will do better.

PREPARE FOR *Tomorrow*

Spend a few moments tonight preparing yourself mentally for your encounter with tomorrow. What will be needed of you? What do you need? Will you be facing a difficult situation that demands some extra self-compassion or self-care?

Sunset MEDITATION

For one week, see if you can watch the sun set each night. What is different about each sunset, and what is the same? What's different about *you* each night, and what is the same? Allow the sunset to be a time to greet the end of the day and transition into rest.

MANTRA

I WELCOME AND SAVOR REST.

MANTRA

I GIVE MYSELF PERMISSION TO NO LONGER BE ON THE GO.

BEDROOM *Retreat*

As it's often the last place you tidy up, take some time today to make your bedroom a nurturing space to retreat to at the end of the day: diffuse some lavender essential oil, light a candle, fluff up your pillows, add a fuzzy blanket to your bed, get a heating pad or hot-water bottle, or just clear out the clutter so you can truly relax at the end of your day.

Silent NIGHT

You may feel like you rarely experience silence. Tonight institute a silent night: no TV, no chores, no email, no catching up on work, no conversation, just silence. Turn down the lights, enjoy a soothing beverage, and savor the quiet solitude.

SLEEP AS *Surrender*

As you climb into bed tonight, remember that sleep is a powerful lesson in surrender: we don't know when and how we will slide from wakefulness into slumber, but we know it will happen. All we can do is create the proper conditions, and then lie down and trust.

Yawn

Go ahead and give in to that yawn at the end of the day. When you pay attention to your yawn, you may realize just how good it feels—it activates the soothing part of your nervous system, releases oxytocin and serotonin, which are feel-good hormones, and helps you feel more relaxed. In fact, just reading this probably makes you want to yawn ... so go ahead.

MANTRA

TOMORROW IS A CHANCE FOR ME TO BEGIN AGAIN.

WHEN YOU *Can't Sleep*

In the *Book of Joy*, the Dalai Lama shares this trick for insomnia: When he can't sleep, he thinks of all the other people throughout the world that, right at that moment, also cannot fall asleep. If you're awake in the wee hours of the night, you can be sure a lot of other people are also up. Being awake in the middle of the night can feel profoundly isolating; see if you can find comfort in knowing that you are not alone.

Five GOOD THINGS

Before you go to bed, list five good things that happened today. You can do this in a journal, or simply tick them off on your fingers. Even the smallest win ("I managed to open the jar at my first attempt") counts!

MANTRA

TODAY WAS HARD. BUT I DID IT AND I AM STRONGER FOR IT.

SLEEP *Meditation*

Before you go to sleep, remember to SLEEP:

Savor: What's one positive thing you want to remember about today?

Learn: What's one thing you learned from today?

Ease: What can you do to bring ease to tomorrow?

Engage: What can you do to bring energy to tomorrow?

Prepare: What do you need to do to be ready for tomorrow?

BEDTIME *Massage*

Give your hard-working body a bit of love before bed—rub some lotion or essential oils on your hands and feet, massage your temples and cheeks and jaw, and gently tend to any aching muscles. Place a warm lavender compress on your forehead, snuggle up to a heating pad, and take a few soothing deep breaths.

Your Mindful Life

With mindfulness, we accept whatever is present.
Because that's WHAT IS.

It's not resignation—it's simply recognizing this is what it's like right now.

And then we have a choice.

If it's something we can change, we can work in the next moment to change it.

If it's something we cannot change, we can choose to soften into it.

Mindfulness doesn't eliminate the stressors from your life. Your loved ones will still throw tantrums, people will still cut you off in traffic, and it may rain sometimes.

The profound transformation takes place within you.
You choose to relate to the stressors in life more skillfully.

And that is LIFE-CHANGING.

YOU'VE GOT THIS!

Resources

WEBSITES

Left Brain Buddha: The Modern Mindful Life
www.leftbrainbuddha.com
Author's blog.

Dr Dan Siegel
www.drdansiegel.com
Resources on mindfulness.

Greater Good Science Center
greatergood.berkeley.edu/topic/mindfulness
Articles and more.

Centre for Mindfulness Practice and Research
www.bangor.ac.uk/mindfulness
Updates on the latest research, including audio meditations.

APPS

Headspace

Happier Meditation

Insight Timer

Calm

Index